About Skill Builders
Grammar

D0061904

Grade 4

Welcome to Skill Builders *Grammar* for fourth grade. This book is designed to improve children's grammar skills through focused practice. This full-color workbook contains grade-level-appropriate activities based on national standards to help ensure that children master basic skills before progressing.

More than 70 pages of activities cover essential grammar skills, such as parts of speech, capitalization, punctuation, and usage. The book's colorful, inviting format, easy-to-follow directions, and clear examples help build children's confidence and make grammar more accessible and enjoyable.

The Skill Builders series offers workbooks that are perfect for keeping skills sharp during the school year or preparing children for the next grade.

Credits:

Content Editors: Nancy Bosse and Elizabeth Swenson
Copy Editor: Julie B. Killian
Layout and Cover Design: Nick Greenwood

www.carsondellosa.com
Carson-Dellosa Publishing LLC
Greensboro, North Carolina

Printed in the USA • All rights reserved.

ISBN 978-1-936023-21-9
02-143111151

Table of Contents

Nouns

Write each noun in the correct category.

> A **noun** is a word that names a person, place, thing, or idea.
>
> Examples: person = scientist, Matthew
> place = kitchen, United States
> thing = bridge, Empire State Building
> idea = joy, freedom

computer	imagination	Neptune	pilot
cucumber	Indian Ocean	South America	playground
friend	love	parent	refrigerator
happiness	Megan	peace	shell

Person

friend, Megan,
parent, pilot,

Place

Indian Ocean,
Neptun, South America,
play ground,

Thing

Cucamber, refrigerator,
shell

Idea

happiness,
imagiation, love,
peace

Common and Proper Nouns

Write each noun in the correct category. Capitalize each proper noun.

A **common noun** names a general person, place, thing, or idea.

Examples: girl, school, mirror, happiness

A **proper noun** names a specific person, place, or thing and begins with a capital letter.

Examples: Betsy Ross, Sears Tower, Niagara Falls

kara	teammate	woman	judge
doctor	carlos perez	artist	independence
ms. prasad	dr. dolby	france	grand canyon
liberty	florida	pacific ocean	river

Common Nouns	**Proper Nouns**
_____	_____
_____	_____
_____	_____
_____	_____
_____	_____
_____	_____
_____	_____
_____	_____

Plural Nouns

Write the plural form of each singular noun.

A **singular noun** names one person, place, thing, or idea.
A **plural noun** names more than one person, place, thing, or idea.

Singular	Plural
1. coach	_____
2. sheep	_____
3. roof	_____
4. mouse	_____
5. donkey	_____
6. shelf	_____
7. class	_____
8. berry	_____

Collective Nouns

Underline each collective noun.

A **collective noun** names a group of similar things, people, or animals. A collective noun is usually treated as a singular noun.

Examples: The <u>audience</u> enjoys our performance tonight.

The <u>herd</u> grazes in the pasture all day long.

1. The flock of geese flies north every year.

2. Our entire class likes that game.

3. The committee accepts our plan.

4. The naval fleet performs exercises at sea this time of year.

5. Coco's litter of puppies sleeps together.

6. The city's orchestra plays beautifully.

7. I hope my team wins its final game!

8. A crowd gathers to hear the results.

Possessive Nouns

Write the correct form of the possessive noun to complete each sentence.

A **possessive noun** shows ownership.

To make a singular noun possessive, add an apostrophe -s ('s).

Examples: **cat's** food   **boss's** pen

To make a plural noun that ends in -s possessive, add an apostrophe (') after the -s.

Examples: **dogs'** collars   **players'** helmets

To make a plural noun that does not end in -s possessive, add an apostrophe -s ('s).

Examples: **men's** shoes   **children's** toys

1. The pond belongs to those frogs. It is the

   _____ pond.

2. Those crayons belong to Marisa. They are

   _____ crayons.

3. These bikes belong to those boys. They are the

   _____ bikes.

4. The car belongs to the neighbors. It is the

   _____ car.

Noun Review

Underline each common noun. Circle each proper noun.

Cheetahs are elegant and graceful. They run at speeds of up to 70 miles (113 kilometers) per hour. The cheetah is the fastest member of the cat family. Cheetahs were once found in Africa, the Middle East, and India. Now, they are mostly found in Africa.

Add an apostrophe (') to each possessive noun.

Cheetahs have long, muscular legs, small heads, and long necks. Cheetahs feet have special pads to help them run. Cheetahs are fast when they run short distances. But, they cannot run quickly for long distances because they get overheated.

Write PL above each plural noun. Write CN above each collective noun.

Cheetahs usually hunt antelopes and hares. Sometimes, a group of cheetahs comes upon a herd of zebras or wildebeests. Although cheetahs are fast, they stay hidden as they approach their prey. Then, they surprise their prey with a burst of speed.

Pronouns

A **pronoun** is a word that takes the place of a noun. A **personal pronoun** refers to a specific person, place, or thing.

Singular Personal Pronouns		Plural Personal Pronouns	
I	her	we	they
me	he	us	them
you	him	you	
she	it		

Example: <u>We</u> hope that <u>he</u> has fun.

1. Kenan and I went to the store.

2. While we were there, we bought groceries for the next week.

3. I asked him to help me choose some food for a special dinner.

4. It would be a surprise dinner for Mom and Dad.

5. They are celebrating an anniversary, and we want it to be very special for them.

Possessive Pronouns

Rewrite the sentences using possessive pronouns to replace the underlined words.

Possessive pronouns replace nouns that show ownership.
Possessive pronouns do not use apostrophes.

Singular Possessive Pronouns		Plural Possessive Pronouns	
my	hers	our	yours
mine	its	ours	their
his	your	your	theirs
her	yours		

Example: The painting is <u>Jenna's</u>.
The painting is **hers**.

---

1. Joanne's chair bumped into <u>my chair</u>.

    _____

2. <u>Holly's</u> book broke <u>Brad's</u> glasses.

    _____

3. Robert borrowed <u>Miguel's</u> markers.

    _____

4. We saw <u>the children's</u> kites flying in the park.

    _____

5. <u>That phone's</u> ring is very loud.

    _____

Pronoun Review

Circle the pronouns in parentheses that correctly complete each sentence.

1. (I, Me) went to (her, hers) house.

2. Can (you, your) come to (our, ours) pool?

3. (He, Him) helped hang (their, theirs) posters.

4. (They, Them) delivered the boxes to (her, hers) office.

5. (She, Her) drew a larger butterfly than (my, mine).

6. (We, Us) will build a tree fort with (our, ours) dad.

7. Will (he, him) have a turn after (mine, mines)?

8. (He, Him) threw the ball to (my, mine) sister.

9. (She, Her) likes my soccer ball better than (her, hers).

10. (His, Him) answers matched (our, ours).

Action Verbs

Underline each action verb.

An **action verb** shows what someone or something does, has done, or will do.

Example: The wind <u>blows</u> the leaves from the tree.

1. The children play hide-and-seek.

2. Zack counts to 50.

3. Everyone hides from Zack.

4. Jan crouches behind the slide.

5. Sam crawls along the fence.

6. Scott jumps over the log.

7. Evelyn giggles behind the oak tree.

8. Joey climbs the old maple tree.

Linking Verbs

Underline each linking verb.

A **linking verb** links the subject to the rest of the sentence. A linking verb does not show action. Some linking verbs are forms of the verb *be*.

Common Linking Verbs

am	are	were
is	was	

Examples: I <u>am</u> nine years old.

We <u>are</u> in fourth grade.

1. An entomologist is a scientist who studies insects.

2. Insects are the most plentiful creatures on the earth.

3. A honeycomb cell is a home for one honeybee egg.

4. Larvae are baby insects that hatch from eggs.

5. Monarchs are migrating butterflies.

6. A moth is different from a butterfly.

7. All ladybugs are not female.

8. Spiders are not insects.

Linking Verbs

Underline each linking verb.

A **linking verb** links the subject to the rest of the sentence. Some linking verbs are forms of the verb *be*.

Other Linking Verbs

appear	become	look	seem	sound
feel	grow	remain	smell	taste

Example: The students <u>seem</u> pleased with their art projects.

1. Several art projects remain on the shelf.

2. Many pots become too hot to touch.

3. That lump of clay appears hard.

4. This ceramic bird seems unusual.

5. Our stone table feels smooth.

6. Your markers smell awful.

7. All of the artwork looks great.

8. Students often become art fans through pottery.

Helping Verbs

Underline each helping verb. Draw an arrow from each helping verb to the verb that it helps.

A **helping verb** helps the main verb by telling more about the time of the action.

Common Helping Verbs

am	are	is
have	has	had
may	must	might
can	could	would
	should	

Example: Sadie is playing the piano in the recital.

1.   This area would make a good picnic spot.

2.   Those crickets are making a lot of noise.

3.   Melissa should eat her sandwich for lunch today.

4.   Quinn might buy a new bike.

5.   Matthew can chop the nuts for the banana bread.

Verb Phrases

Underline each verb phrase once. Then, underline each main verb again.

A **verb phrase** contains a main verb and one or more helping verbs.

Examples: The swimming instructor is <u>giving</u> lessons today.

The team has been <u>training</u> for several weeks.

1. Maurice had learned the backstroke last summer.

2. Isabella and Emma are practicing for the meet.

3. The competition will be held at Arrowhead Pool.

4. Our coach is driving the team to the meet.

5. Everyone was packed in the van.

6. I am competing in the 4 × 100m relay race.

7. Norman should win the competition.

8. Valerie could win her first medal.

Past- and Present-Tense Verbs

Underline each verb. Then, write _PR_ if the verb is in the present tense or _PA_ if the verb is in the past tense.

> The tense of a verb tells _when_ the action happens. A **present-tense verb** expresses an action that is happening now. A **past-tense verb** expresses an action that happened earlier.
>
> Most verbs form the past tense by adding _-ed_.
>
> Examples: I smile when I watch that show. (_PR_)
>
> I smiled when I watched that show. (_PA_)

1. The sea horse floats by the starfish. _____

2. Neil watched the sleeping hamster. _____

3. The kites dance in the breeze. _____

4. Sean sharpens his pencil. _____

5. Natalie bandaged her finger. _____

6. We tumble down the sand dune. _____

7. Cameron flicked the paper football. _____

8. Ahmad designed a snow fort. _____

Irregular Verbs

Write the past tense of each irregular verb.

Irregular verbs do not add -ed to form the past tense.

Examples: I **see** the red car. (present tense)

I **saw** the red car yesterday. (past tense)

Present Tense	Past Tense	Present Tense	Past Tense
1. write	_____	2. teach	_____
3. draw	_____	4. find	_____
5. speak	_____	6. feel	_____
7. hold	_____	8. bend	_____
9. hear	_____	10. catch	_____
11. throw	_____	12. go	_____

Irregular Verbs

Write the past tense of the verb in parentheses to correctly complete each sentence.

> Examples: My father **teaches** third grade this year.
> (present tense)
> My father **taught** third grade last year.
> (past tense)

1. Pablo (do) _____ his best work today.

2. The quarterback (run) _____ for a touchdown.

3. Addie (take) _____ a walk along the riverfront.

4. After breakfast, Trenton (go) _____ for a ride.

5. Our new puppy (sleep) _____ all night long.

6. Vanessa (begin) _____ a new book today.

7. The little boy (wear) _____ a hole in his socks.

8. This airplane (fly) _____ from Miami to Toronto.

Future-Tense Verbs

Underline each present-tense verb. Then, rewrite each sentence in the future tense.

The tense of a verb tells *when* the action happens. A **future-tense verb** expresses an action that is going to happen in the future. The helping verb *will* is added before the main verb to form the future tense.

If the noun is singular, the *-s* ending of the verb is dropped before adding *will*.

Examples: Dad <u>mows</u> the lawn. (present tense)

Dad <u>will mow</u> the lawn. (future tense)

1. I take piano lessons.

   _____

   _____

2. Ivan comes to my house on Saturdays.

   _____

   _____

3. You are the line leader today.

   _____

   _____

Verb Tense Review

Underline each verb or verb phrase. Then, circle the correct verb tense for each underlined verb.

1. Gabe signed his name on the card.

   present   past   future

2. Greg will golf in the tournament.

   present   past   future

3. Anthony snaps the links together.

   present   past   future

4. Brantley climbs into his bed.

   present   past   future

5. Lamar will set his alarm clock.

   present   past   future

6. Kellie rocked her puppy to sleep.

   present   past   future

Noun or Verb

Write _N_ if the underlined word or words is a noun or _V_ if the underlined word or words is a verb.

Sometimes a word that is a noun in one sentence can be a different part of speech in another sentence. How the word is used in a sentence determines its part of speech.

Examples: My mom saw a <u>duck</u> in the park. (noun)

Make sure you <u>duck</u> when you enter the tree house. (verb)

1. Julia wore her birthstone <u>ring</u>. _____

2. <u>Ring</u> the bell to announce dinner. _____

3. The little boy <u>can dress</u> himself. _____

4. The <u>dress</u> had blue stripes. _____

5. He <u>will paint</u> a landscape scene. _____

6. Chang prefers the green <u>paint</u>. _____

7. The surfer rode the <u>wave</u>. _____

8. The child <u>will wave</u> good-bye. _____

Adjectives

Underline each adjective. Then, draw an arrow from each adjective to the noun that it describes.

An **adjective** is a word that describes a noun. Adjectives tell *which one*, *what kind*, or *how many*.

Examples: The <u>dirty</u> puppy needs a bath.

The <u>public</u> library is closed today.

1. Dylan opened the large, wrapped package.

2. Many tiny ants crawled along the fallen tree.

3. Some bothersome mosquitoes are near the screen door.

4. Dawson removed both dirty socks and two muddy shoes.

5. One spotted dalmatian rode on the noisy, red fire engine.

6. Seth used the sharp scissors to cut the thick, brown paper.

7. Justin squeezed two tart lemons for lemonade.

8. Molly ate a large, red apple.

Adjectives

Write an adjective for each category. Use a different adjective each time. The first one has been done for you.

Noun	Which one?	What kind?	How many?
plant	green	tropical	one
1. gorilla	_____	_____	_____
2. cookies	_____	_____	_____
3. toy	_____	_____	_____
4. costume	_____	_____	_____
5. planet	_____	_____	_____
6. volcano	_____	_____	_____
7. mountains	_____	_____	_____
8. lizard	_____	_____	_____
9. dog	_____	_____	_____
10. tree	_____	_____	_____

Articles

Write the articles that correctly complete the passage.

A, *an*, and *the* are adjectives that are called **articles**.

Use *a* before a word that begins with a consonant sound.

Use *an* before a word that begins with a vowel sound.

Use *the* if the noun is plural or names a particular person, place, or thing.

Example: **A** crocodile and **an** elephant posed for **the** photographer.

African parrots live in tropical areas. One variety

is _____ rose-ringed parakeet. This type of parakeet

has _____ extremely long tail, _____ bright red bill, and

_____ bright green head. _____ nine species of lovebirds

are _____ only small African parrots. _____ lovebirds

have short, rounded tails and rather large bills. _____

lovebirds got that name because they were believed to mate for

life. _____ large, gray parrot from _____ West African rain

forest is _____ popular pet because this type of parrot can

learn to say words.

Adjectives That Compare

Complete the chart for each adjective.

A **comparative adjective** compares two nouns or pronouns. The comparative form is made by adding -er to most adjectives.

Example: This apple is **sweeter** than that one. (comparative)

A **superlative adjective** compares three or more nouns or pronouns. The superlative form is made by adding -est to most adjectives.

Example: This apple is the **sweetest** one I have had. (superlative)

Adjective	Comparative	Superlative
1. old	_____	_____
2. soft	_____	_____
3. loud	_____	_____
4. short	_____	_____
5. small	_____	_____

Comparative and Superlative Adjectives

Write the correct form of the adjective in parentheses to complete each sentence.

> When an adjective contains three or more syllables, use the word *more* or *most* before the adjective instead of adding *-er* or *-est*.
>
> Examples: Fact can be **more interesting** than fiction. (comparative)
> New York is one of North America's **most interesting** cities. (superlative)

1. In Louisiana, New Orleans is a _____ tourist city than Baton Rouge. (popular)

2. It is also one of the world's _____ sports. (valuable)

3. Boulder, Colorado, is _____ than New Orleans. (elevated)

4. Several of New Orleans' _____ structures border Jackson Square. (enormous)

5. Of all the restaurants, we were _____ with the locally owned ones. (impressed)

Adjective Review

Underline each adjective. Then, draw an arrow to the noun that each adjective describes.

1. Chocolate ice cream is a popular dessert.

2. The large, yellow school bus is filled with excited children.

3. I saw a white rabbit in the front yard.

4. I took a delicious lasagna to an ill neighbor.

5. The art fair displayed amazing drawings.

6. A funny movie entertained the four young children.

7. Al liked the fancy, red shoes with black and white ribbons.

8. Shane drove the rusty, old truck in the heavy rain.

9. A lovely white house is at the end of a long, bumpy road.

10. He listened as large raindrops hit the old, metal roof.

Noun, Verb, or Adjective?

Write *noun*, *verb*, or *adjective* to identify each underlined word.

A word that is a used as a noun in one sentence can be used as a verb or an adjective in another sentence. How the word is used in a sentence determines its part of speech.

Examples: That <u>fly</u> is bothering me. (noun)
 I <u>fly</u> my kite. (verb)
 Sarah caught the <u>fly</u> ball. (adjective)

1. Logan will iron his <u>wrinkled</u> pants. _____

2. Jayla <u>wrinkled</u> her nose at the smell. _____

3. The <u>ship</u> is docked at the pier. _____

4. Luke will <u>ship</u> the package today. _____

5. I used <u>liquid</u> soap to wash the dishes. _____

6. This <u>liquid</u> will pour easily. _____

7. Lauren <u>paints</u> many things. _____

8. Katie bought a new set of <u>paints</u>. _____

Adverbs

Underline each adverb. Then, draw an arrow from each adverb to the verb that it describes.

An **adverb** is a word that describes a verb. It tells *how, when,* or *where* something happens.

Many adverbs end in *-ly.*

Example: The dancer glided <u>gracefully</u> across the stage.

1. Jordan closed the book quickly.

2. Tyrone frequently plays in the park.

3. Zane worked quietly on his model.

4. Leo jogged slowly along the path.

5. Nikki mixed the ingredients thoroughly.

6. They will unwrap the dishes carefully.

7. The fragile package arrived safely.

8. Bashfully, Shauna smiled for the camera.

Adverbs

Underline each adverb. Then, draw an arrow from each adverb to the verb that it describes.

> Some adverbs do not end in -ly.
>
> ### Adverbs
>
> always   later   now   very
>
> earlier   never   soon   yesterday
>
> Example: James went to the park yesterday.

1.   The moving company had arrived early to begin packing.

2.   The children were very excited to see the moving truck.

3.   The movers stopped often to tape the boxes.

4.   One mover walked backward with some boxes.

5.   Now, the moving truck was packed.

6.   It will arrive at the new house tonight.

7.   The children will sleep in their new house tomorrow.

8.   Their parents will unpack the smaller boxes later.

Adverbs That Compare

Write the correct form of the adverb in parentheses to complete each sentence.

A **comparative adverb** compares two actions. The comparative form is made by adding -er to some adverbs.

Example: The jet is **faster** than the plane. (comparative)

A **superlative adverb** compares more than two actions. The superlative form is made by adding -est to some adverbs.

Example: That jet is the **fastest** one at the airport. (superlative)

If an adverb ends in -ly or has more than one syllable, the word more or most is added before the adverb.

Example: Jennifer typed **more quickly** than Michelle, but Pedro typed **most quickly** of all.

1. Lamonte slept _____ than Jonathan. (late)

2. The bird flew _____ than the moth. (gracefully)

3. Li climbed the _____ of all the players. (high)

4. The gem sparkled _____ than the stones. (brilliantly)

5. Coach Mori whistled _____ than the other coach. (loud)

Adjective or Adverb?

Underline the word in parentheses that correctly completes each sentence.

Adjectives	Adverbs
good (always an adjective)	well (means done effectively)
bad	badly
real (means true or genuine)	really (means very)
sure (means reliable)	surely (means definitely)

1. Jeff plays basketball (good, well).

2. The detective (sure, surely) solved the mystery.

3. Kelsey is a (real, really) hero to the community.

4. Everyone had a (good, well) time at the picnic.

5. Our team lost (bad, badly) at the state finals.

6. The (bad, badly) storm destroyed the peach crop.

7. John felt (real, really) dizzy after riding the roller coaster.

8. Sierra was the (sure, surely) choice for the job.

Adverb Review

Underline each adverb. Then, draw an arrow to the word or words that it modifies.

1. Leaves were scattered everywhere.

2. The speech was extremely long.

3. Place the toy box here.

4. Complete your homework carefully and accurately.

Write the correct form of the word in parentheses to complete each sentence.

5. Noah sang _____ in the chorus. (beautiful)

6. Garrick skates _____ than his brother. (fast)

7. Tara _____ introduced her teacher. (polite)

8. Our collie barked the _____ of all of the dogs. (loud)

Prepositions

Underline each preposition.

A **preposition** is a word that tells about a noun's location or position.

Example: The box came <u>in</u> the mail <u>with</u> this note.

Common Prepositions

around	by	from	in
of	to	under	with

1. Maddie would like a cup of hot chocolate.

2. That car beside the restaurant is ours.

3. Kristen found her pencil under the couch.

4. The pretzels in the jar are delicious.

5. This letter from my grandmother came last night.

6. The seat in the middle is Jose's.

7. Casey saw a goldfish with five black spots.

8. A huge bump in the snow sent the sled flying.

Prepositional Phrases

Underline each prepositional phrase.

A **prepositional phrase** is a group of words that begins with a preposition and ends with a noun.

Example: The squirrels in our yard ran up the tree.

1. Ben and Claire walked to school.

2. The birds built a nest in the tree.

3. The bird feeder above the fence attracted many birds.

4. We recognized the car from our neighborhood.

5. Our small, tan puppy played under the porch behind our house.

6. Trevor and I wrapped the prizes for the event.

7. Tony passed the carrots to his mom.

8. Please put an umbrella in the trunk.

Preposition Review

Underline each prepositional phrase in the passage.

Bats are the only flying mammals. They are the hunters of the night sky. Bats use a built-in system called echolocation while navigating through the sky, even in the dark. They also use it to locate food on the ground and in the air. When bats migrate, they fly as high as 10,000 feet (3,000 meters) or more.

A bat's wings are very helpful. A bat can scoop things with her wings. She can cradle a baby bat in the bottom of her wing. A bat can wrap her wings around herself like a blanket. A bat will also flip food into her own mouth, using her wings as a slingshot.

Bats can hibernate at any time. If food is scarce, bats will hibernate until better times come along. Where bats hang is not random. Each bat has her own space. Bats usually hang near a cave entrance. Bats often return to the same cave where they were born.

Conjunctions

Rewrite each sentence pair as one sentence using a comma and a conjunction.

A **conjunction** combines sentences that have similar or related ideas.

Examples: Kim eats her sandwich. She does not eat her carrots. (two sentences)

Kim eats her sandwich, **but** she does not eat her carrots. (one sentence)

Common Conjunctions

and	but	for	nor
or	so	yet	

1. Ava slept on the plane. She did not sleep on the train.

   _____

2. The pencil is old. The eraser is new.

   _____

3. Aidan plays basketball. Taylor plays tennis.

   _____

4. The pillow is soft. The blanket is scratchy.

   _____

5. Amira finished her math. She did not finish her reading.

   _____

Parts of Speech Review

Identify the part of speech for each underlined word. Write **N** for noun, **PRO** for pronoun, **V** for verb, **ADJ** for adjective, **ADV** for adverb, **PREP** for preposition, or **CONJ** for conjunction.

1. An adult insect has <u>three</u> body sections. _____

2. The head of an insect contains eyes, antennae, <u>and</u> a mouth. _____

3. An insect's eyes <u>are</u> often compound. _____

4. The different types of mouthparts <u>determine</u> how an insect will eat. _____

5. Insects use antennae to detect odors <u>in</u> the air. _____

6. The thorax is the <u>middle</u> section of an adult insect. _____

7. Each segment of the thorax <u>has</u> one pair of legs. _____

8. Altogether, <u>they</u> have six legs. _____

Parts of Speech Review

Use the key to number each word. Then, write each set of words in the correct order to form a sentence.

1 = article	2 = adjective	3 = noun
4 = verb	5 = adverb	

Example: 3   4   2   1   5
           apple fell red a quietly

           1 2   3   4   5
           A red apple fell quietly.

1. barked big dog loudly the

    _____

2. very happy smiled woman a

    _____

3. huge cautiously airplane the landed

    _____

4. high orange an bounced ball

    _____

5. beautifully large played orchestra the

    _____

Sentences

Write _S_ if the group of words is a sentence. Write _F_ if the group of words is a fragment.

> A **sentence** is a group of words that expresses a complete thought. A complete sentence has a subject that tells _who_ or _what_ the sentence is about and a verb or verb phrase that tells _what happens_.
>
> Example: Ran home quickly. (sentence fragment)
>   Bill ran home quickly. (complete sentence)

1. _____ Mrs. Chang has a lovely garden.

2. _____ The large cat purred loudly.

3. _____ Mariah cried because the movie was sad.

4. _____ Drove to the park in the afternoon.

5. _____ Kelly dug up the weeds.

6. _____ Hau replaced the floor in the kitchen.

7. _____ Lisa, the manager, at the toy store.

8. _____ The library near our house.

Simple Subjects

Underline the simple subject of each sentence.

The **simple subject** is the main word that tells *who* or *what* a sentence is about. The simple subject can be a noun or a pronoun.

Example: A small, spotted <u>fish</u> swam slowly around the pond.

1. The suspension bridge spans across the river.

2. Rick's shoelace is untied again.

3. My cousin from Idaho visited Oregon.

4. Diamonds are compressed coal.

5. My dad mowed the lawn last Saturday.

6. That list helps me remember things.

7. Our leaky sink needs to be fixed.

8. Marcus plays tennis at the community center.

Subject Pronouns

Write a subject pronoun to replace each underlined word or group of words.

The subject of a sentence tells *what* or *whom* the sentence is about. A **subject pronoun** can be the subject of a sentence.

Only these pronouns can be used as the subject of a sentence:

I	he	we
you	she	you
	it	they

Example: Dr. Yu and Dr. Santos are planning a trip to Africa.
They are planning a trip to Africa.

1. Dr. Yu and I studied the hippos. _____

2. Dr. Yu watched the hippos play in the water. _____

3. The hippos spent the day in the water. _____

4. When hippos go underwater, their noses close. _____

5. The mother hippo protects her babies. _____

Simple Predicates

Underline each simple predicate.

The **simple predicate** is always a verb. A simple predicate contains the main verb and any helping verbs.

Examples: Caden <u>has kicked</u> the winning goal.
Caden <u>is</u> an excellent soccer player.

1. Fiona scrunched up her nose.

2. Jacob bounced on his bed.

3. Emily rustled the bag of pretzels.

4. Nassim will be in my fourth-grade class.

5. The swan paddled in the pond.

6. Alvin has written the date on his paper.

7. The pudding splattered all over the floor.

8. Jack ate a cheese sandwich.

Simple Subjects and Predicates

Underline each simple subject once. Underline each simple predicate twice.

Example: The brown <u>bears</u> <u><u>were hibernating</u></u>.

1. Yellowstone is the oldest U.S. national park.

2. The park has many hot springs and geysers.

3. Grizzly bears and bison can be found there.

4. Thousands of visitors come to Yellowstone each year.

5. My family camped there last year.

6. We enjoyed the beautiful mountains.

7. My brother saw a huge bug in the dirt.

8. We will visit Yosemite National Park next summer.

Complete Subjects

Underline each complete subject. Circle each simple subject.

> The **complete subject** contains the simple subject and any words that describe the subject.
>
> Example: The (cup) of hot chocolate was on the table.

1.   That puppy by the bench dug a big hole.

2.   One canoe near the dock had a small hole in it.

3.   This parrot with the green head belongs to Gabriel.

4.   The brown mare brushed my shoulder with her nose.

5.   Several slimy earthworms are in that pile of leaves.

6.   The open garbage can smells awful.

7.   Frogs will swim in this pond in the spring.

8.   Our crackling campfire burned brightly.

Complete Predicates

Underline each complete predicate. Circle each simple predicate.

The **complete predicate** contains the simple predicate and any adverbs or other words that tell *where, when, why,* or *how* about the verb.

Any words in a sentence that are not part of the complete subject are part of the complete predicate.

Examples: Dion (will bike) to the beach.

Candice and her cousin (play) the piano beautifully.

1. The spilled juice may stain Heather's shoes.

2. Two tiny owlets hoot softly for a meal.

3. Paige and Juan guard the goals.

4. Miranda fills the bird feeder every week.

5. The squirrels will gather all of the nuts from that tree.

6. Nellie quickly subtracts a page of math problems.

7. Kevin carefully sews the button on his jacket.

8. Our family will attend the ceremony next Tuesday.

Complete Subjects and Predicates Review

Underline each complete subject once. Underline each complete predicate twice.

1. Dustin's noisy movie distracted Krystal from her work.

2. The box of tissues was emptied quickly.

3. That old, rusty swing continues to be the children's favorite.

4. Tyler loaded the back of the truck with plants.

5. Some shiny marbles were scattered across the tile floor.

6. Many important men signed the Declaration of Independence.

7. Few tomato plants will survive the early morning frost.

8. Three steep cliffs towered above the river.

9. A remote-controlled car raced along the sidewalk.

10. The giant toad ate many insects.

Object Pronouns

Write an object pronoun to replace each underlined word or group of words.

An **object pronoun** takes the place of a noun in the predicate. An object pronoun receives the action of the verb. It usually comes after the verb or preposition.

Common Object Pronouns

me	her	us	you
him	you	it	them

Example: Grace helped her brother.
Grace helped **him**.

1. Darron sent a package to Blake and Hailey. _____

2. Mrs. Marino read the book to Will and me. _____

3. Spencer spoke on the phone with Dante. _____

4. The basketball swished through the hoop. _____

5. Sage biked to the park with Jessica. _____

6. Jasper handed the shovel to Timothy. _____

Compound Subjects

Underline each compound subject. Circle each conjunction.

A **compound subject** is formed when two or more subjects are joined by conjunctions such as *and* or *or*.

Example: Florida (and) California are popular tourist states.

1. Daytona Beach, Fort Lauderdale, and Miami are popular seaside vacation spots.

2. Tourists and residents enjoy vacationing in the Sunshine State.

3. Florida's population and industry are growing rapidly.

4. Many farmers, miners, and fishermen work in Florida.

5. Beaches, a warm climate, and mineral deposits are some of Florida's natural resources.

6. Oranges, grapefruits, and tangerines are examples of the citrus fruits grown in Florida.

7. Several famous theme parks and water parks are located in Florida.

8. The Atlantic Ocean and the Gulf of Mexico border the Florida peninsula.

Compound Predicates

Underline each compound predicate. Circle each conjunction.

> A **compound predicate** is formed when a sentence has two or more predicates joined by conjunctions such as *and* or *or*.
>
> Example: Thousands of visitors <u>swim (and) play</u> there.
>   (compound predicate)

1. Olivia walked and marched in the parade.

2. Grey took hold of the rope and climbed it.

3. Several monkeys climbed the tree and jumped on the branches.

4. Ty grabbed his backpack and ran for the door.

5. The mice scurried and hid.

6. Mia ran across the mat and flipped.

7. Peanuts fell on the floor and rolled.

8. The club members played games and sang songs.

Subject and Verb Agreement

Underline the verb in parentheses that correctly completes each sentence.

Subjects and verbs in a sentence must agree with each other in number. If the subject is singular, the verb must be singular.

Examples: A computer **works** faster than a typewriter.
Computers **work** faster than typewriters.

1. A severe thunderstorm (cause, causes) many problems.

2. Puddles (form, forms) after a rainstorm.

3. Lightning (strike, strikes) during a thunderstorm.

4. The damage from a storm (create, creates) problems for the power company.

5. During a drought, people (rejoice, rejoices) when rain is in the forecast.

6. That puppy always (bark, barks) when it hears thunder.

7. Floods (occur, occurs) sometimes after a bad storm.

8. A thunderstorm (ruin, ruins) a picnic.

Subject Pronoun and Verb Agreement

Underline the verb in parentheses that correctly completes each sentence.

Subject pronouns and verbs in a sentence must agree with each other in number. If the subject pronoun is singular, the verb must be singular.

Examples: **He** helps my aunt, and **I** help my uncle.
They appreciate the gifts.

1. She (want, wants) to be a scientist.

2. They (jump, jumps) on the trampoline.

3. I (wonder, wonders) how he did all of that work.

4. We (live, lives) in South Dakota.

5. He (know, knows) a lot about writing books.

6. It (use, uses) a lot of gas.

7. You (write, writes) very neatly.

8. They (enjoy, enjoys) films about wildlife.

Verb Endings

Write the correct form of the verb in parentheses to complete each sentence.

To agree with a singular subject, most present-tense verbs add -s.

If	Then	Example
a verb ends with -sh, -s, -z, -ch, or -x	add -es to the end	(pitch, pitches)
a verb ends with a consonant -y	change -y to -i and add -es	(try, tries)
a verb ends with a vowel -y	add -s	(enjoy, enjoys)

1. Hannah _____ on a carrot. (munch)

2. Amber _____ her kite. (fly)

3. Tia _____ her bike. (fix)

4. Beth _____ the dishes on the table. (lay)

5. Wren _____ to catch the ball. (hurry)

6. Paul _____ like a bee. (buzz)

7. Maria _____ her brother to tie his shoes. (teach)

8. Vince _____ the piano. (play)

Compound Subject and Verb Agreement

Underline the verb in parentheses that correctly completes each sentence.

Compound subjects and verbs in a sentence must agree with each other in number. A compound subject is treated as a plural subject. The verb must be plural.

Examples: Jai <u>likes</u> milk. Trey <u>likes</u> milk.
Jai and Trey <u>like</u> milk.

1. The teddy bear and the doll (sit, sits) on her pillow.

2. Casey and Carter (slide, slides) down the hill.

3. The lion and the tiger (is, are) pacing.

4. The gray car and the white van (was, were) washed today.

5. A horsefly and a mosquito (fly, flies) through the open door.

6. A large snail and a little goldfish (live, lives) in this aquarium.

7. The hot tub and the pool (is, are) empty.

8. Ahmad and Gavin (enjoy, enjoys) checkers.

Predicate Adjectives

Underline each predicate adjective. Draw an arrow from each predicate adjective to the noun that it describes.

A **predicate adjective** is an adjective that follows a linking verb. A predicate adjective is part of the predicate, but it describes the subject.

Example: This cave is gigantic.

1. This book about tropical islands sounds interesting.

2. The aromas from the kitchen smell wonderful.

3. That huge tractor is muddy.

4. After the sack race, all three children seem tired.

5. The old, rusty trailer is empty.

6. Our homemade pizza dough feels squishy.

7. Ana looks sleepy.

8. Aaron's pottery class is fun.

Contractions

Write the contraction for each word pair.

A **contraction** is a word formed from two words. One or more of the letters are left out when the words are joined. An apostrophe (') takes the place of the missing letters.

Examples: is not = isn't   she will = she'll

            it is = it's   we are = we're

           I have = I've   he would = he'd

1. I + will = _____

2. he + is = _____

3. they + are = _____

4. they + have = _____

5. you + will = _____

6. she + has = _____

7. I + had = _____

8. they + would = _____

Contractions

Write the two words that form each underlined contraction.

Example: I've purchased a new computer.   I have

1. I'm taking a class to learn how to create Web sites.

   _____

2. You're never going to believe what I learned in class!

   _____

3. They're taking a class to learn how to use the Internet.

   _____

4. You'd better find a computer so that you can use e-mail.

   _____

5. I've received 14 e-mails since Tuesday.

   _____

6. Myla said that she's happy with her new monitor.

   _____

Double Negatives

Underline the word in parentheses that correctly completes each sentence.

> A **double negative** is an error caused by using two negative words together in a sentence.
>
> Examples: **Aren't none** of those books on the shelf? (double negative)
>
> **Aren't any** of those books on the shelf? (correct)

1. Becky wasn't (ever, never) going to believe that story.

2. Cory couldn't go (nowhere, anywhere) until he finished his chores.

3. I do not think that (no one, anyone) is hiding in the closet.

4. Poetry wasn't (never, ever) Brayden's favorite thing to read.

5. Elizabeth couldn't find (anything, nothing) in the drawer.

6. I called, but nobody (was, wasn't) home today.

7. Isn't (anyone, no one) going to Mandy's party?

8. We don't have (no, any) time to finish this.

Four Types of Sentences and Ending Punctuation

Write *D* for each declarative sentence, *IN* for each interrogative sentence, *IM* for each imperative sentence, or *E* for each exclamatory sentence. Then, write the correct ending punctuation for each sentence.

Four Types of Sentences	Function	Ending Punctuation
declarative sentence	makes a statement	period
interrogative sentence	asks a question	question mark
imperative sentence	gives a command	period or exclamation point
exclamatory sentence	shows strong feeling	exclamation point

1. _____ Stephen, where are you going

2. _____ Stand next to your desk

3. _____ Erica jogs five miles (eight kilometers) every day

4. _____ I cannot wait to see the movie

5. _____ Did Evan tell you what is in the package

Capitalization

Write the correct capital letter above each word that should be capitalized.

A capital letter is used for the first word in a sentence, proper nouns, the pronoun *I*, and important words in titles of books, movies, and songs.

          T   I   R

Example: the capital of italy is rome.

1. one of the greatest scientists of all time was albert einstein.

2. einstein was born in ulm, germany.

3. in 1909, einstein became a professor at the university of zurich.

4. he was also a professor at a university in prague.

5. albert einstein visited england and the united states.

6. in 1940, einstein became an american citizen.

7. he began teaching in princeton, new jersey.

8. albert einstein wrote a book called *ideas and opinions*.

Capitalization of Proper Nouns

Underline each word that should begin with a capital letter.

A capital letter is used to begin the names of holidays, special events, days of the week, months of the year, geographic locations, and periods in history.

Examples: Memorial Day   Thursday   July

    Mount McKinley   the Middle Ages

1. the lewis and clark expedition explored what is now the northwestern united states.

2. the men planned an expedition to chart a route to the pacific ocean.

3. in may 1804, their expedition began from camp dubois.

4. an indian guide named sacagawea traveled thousands of miles with lewis and clark.

5. they journeyed up the missouri river and across the rocky mountains.

6. next, the group traveled along the columbia river.

Capitalization of Names, Titles, and Nationalities

Rewrite the names, titles, and nationalities using capitalization where needed.

A capital letter is used to begin the first and last names of people. A capital letter is also used to begin a title that comes before a person's name. Proper adjectives, such as nationalities, also are capitalized.

Examples: President Lincoln   Admiral Farragut   Canadian

1. mr. benjamin franklin _____

2. mexican-american festival_____

3. european continent _____

4. dr. john kaplan _____

5. italian leather coat _____

6. mrs. tanaka _____

7. english muffins _____

8. captain sam chadwick _____

More Capitalization of Names

Rewrite each sentence using capitalization where needed.

Words that show family relationship are capitalized when they come before a person's name. If a family relationship word is used by itself in place of a person's name, it is also capitalized. Otherwise, it is lowercased.

Examples: **Mom** wrote a letter to **Uncle** Charlie.
My **mom** wrote a letter to my **uncle**.

Initials that take the place of a name are capitalized and followed by a period.

Example: **E. B.** White

1. aunt jackie recently bought a new car.

   _____

2. john f. kennedy was the youngest U.S. president.

   _____

3. Saturday, dad and i camped in yosemite national park.

   _____

4. My favorite author is c. s. lewis.

   _____

Commas

Write commas where needed in each sentence.

A **comma** (,) is used to separate three or more words or groups of words in a series.

Examples: Shannon, Shay, and Trent worked together on the project.

I walked the dog, took out the trash, and set the table.

A comma is used between the name of a city and its state, province, or country. A comma is also used after the name of the state, province, or country within a sentence.

Example: Delia flew from Paris, France, to Dallas, Texas.

1. Nina Ian Kori and I rode the bus.

2. Her pen pal lives in Olympia Washington.

3. Our yogurt choices are cherry strawberry peach or banana.

4. Kim washed her face brushed her teeth and combed her hair.

5. Mark was born in Halifax Nova Scotia.

6. Carrots lettuce spinach and cucumbers are in the salad.

Commas with Dates

Write commas where needed in each sentence.

A **comma** (,) is used between the date of the month and the year. A comma is also used to separate the day from the month. Commas are also used after the year within a sentence.

Examples: January 4, 2011   Tuesday, January 4

Her recital is Tuesday, January 4, 2011, at 6:00.

1. Alaska became a state on January 3 1959.

2. On May 26 2010 I went on a trip to Peru.

3. The band is performing on Friday June 2.

4. My grandparents were married on June 26 1971.

5. Trisha was born on Sunday January 6 2002.

6. Lee started kindergarten on Tuesday August 27.

7. Bailey will graduate on June 10 2020 with an English degree.

8. The program will be on Thursday February 15.

Commas with Adjectives

Write commas where needed in each sentence.

> A **comma** (,) is used to separate two or more adjectives that describe the same noun.
>
> Example: A broken, red cup sat on the old, wooden table.

1. The huge green house on Grant Lane is vacant.

2. Jeremy and Jay are talented experienced professional skaters.

3. Mom cooked a delicious nutritious dinner.

4. Finishing this project will be a long complicated process.

5. The shipmates watched the dull gloomy sky.

6. The creative energetic young drummer was the crowd favorite.

7. The high fluffy white clouds filled the clear blue summer sky.

8. After our long exciting vacation, we returned to our peaceful quiet neighborhood.

Quotation Marks with Titles

Write quotation marks where needed in each sentence.

Quotation marks (" ") are used before and after the titles of magazine articles, newspaper articles, songs, and poems. Quotation marks also are used around the chapter titles of a book. Book titles do not use quotation marks. Book titles are underlined. If a quotation mark is at the end of a sentence, the period goes inside the quotation marks.

Examples: I read "Drums Are Beating" in today's newspaper. (article)

"Flying to the Moon" is a chapter in Space Travels. (chapter)

We sang "Row, Row, Row Your Boat." (song)

1. Summertime is a chapter in the book A Year with Me.

2. I want to read No Bikes Allowed in today's newspaper.

3. The headline on this page says Meteor Shower Tonight.

4. Irene played Marching Along on her flute.

5. Zeb's favorite song is High Hopes.

6. I love the poem When Stars Come Out.

Quotation Marks with Dialogue

Write quotation marks where needed in each sentence.

Quotation marks are used before and after the exact words that a person says. A comma is usually used to introduce the spoken words. If a quotation mark is at the end of a sentence, the punctuation goes before the quotation mark. A comma or question mark is also used before the closing quotation mark within a sentence.

Examples: Mrs. Huber said, "You are a good writer."
"Call me later if you can," Leigh said.
"May I take a message?" Harry asked.

1. Please wait for me, Nicholas said.

2. Josh said, I think you should enter the contest.

3. Liza asked, What is your phone number?

4. Dad said, Travis is at the recreation center today.

5. When will the parade begin? asked the excited children.

6. The toddler said, Please read me a story.

7. May I speak with Mrs. Jung? the caller asked.

8. The salesperson explained, This will just take a minute.

Homophones

Circle the homophones in parentheses that correctly complete each sentence.

> **Homophones** are words that are pronounced the same but have different spellings and different meanings.
>
> Examples: to, too, two   by, bye, buy   hour, our
>   week, weak   knew, new   write, right
>   way, weigh   here, hear
>   their, there, they're

1. (There, Their, They're) will be basketball tryouts next (weak, week).

2. The teenager went to (by, bye, buy) some (knew, new) clothes.

3. These will (way, weigh) more if (there, their, they're) wet.

4. The show will begin (write, right) at (ate, eight) o'clock.

5. The performance will last (one, won) or (to, too, two) (ours, hours).

Homophones

Write the homophone in parentheses that correctly completes each sentence.

1. The class has _____ own water fountain. (its, it's)

2. Khalil looked _____ the window. (threw, through)

3. Elizabeth wanted the _____ apple. (whole, hole)

4. _____ place is on the bottom of the shelf. (Its, It's)

5. Victor _____ a letter to his mom. (sent, cent, scent)

6. Audrey _____ the winning pass. (threw, through)

7. A penny is the same as one _____ . (sent, cent, scent)

8. _____ too cold to go swimming in the pool. (Its, It's)

9. I like the _____ of that flower. (sent, cent, scent)

10. There is a _____ in my favorite sock. (whole, hole)

Goofy Grammar 1

Write a word for each part of speech below. Then, use the words to complete the activity on page 73.

1. common noun _____

2. adjective _____

3. verb (present tense) _____

4. common noun (place) _____

5. verb (present tense) _____

6. proper noun (place) _____

7. verb (past tense) _____

8. collective noun _____

9. verb (present tense) _____

10. common noun (plural) _____

11. common noun (plural) _____

12. adjective _____

13. common noun _____

14. possessive pronoun _____

15. proper noun (name) _____

16. common noun (plural) _____

Goofy Grammar 1

Use the numbered words you wrote on page 72 to complete the story.

Once upon a time lived a big, green, fire-breathing

_____. His name was Al. Now, Al was

1

very _____. All that Al did all day long

2

was _____ in his _____ and

3   4

_____, except for his occasional trips into

5

_____ to find food. When Al _____ into

6   7

the forest, he would see birds flying in their _____

8

and families of rabbits hopping along together. This just

made him _____. Al longed for family and

9

_____. This was a problem because of his fire

10

breathing. Most _____ wanted nothing to do with Al.

11

That is until one day when a large, _____,

12

fire-breathing _____ came along. _____

13   14

name was _____. They both knew that they were

15

going to be good _____. They also knew that they

16

were meant to be friends forever.

Goofy Grammar 2

Write a word for each part of speech below. Then, use the words to complete the activity on page 75.

1. common noun _____

2. adjective _____

3. adjective _____

4. adjective _____

5. common noun (place) _____

6. common noun (place) _____

7. common noun (plural) _____

8. adverb _____

9. common noun _____

10. verb _____

11. common noun _____

12. common noun _____

13. adjective _____

14. adjective _____

Goofy Grammar 2

Use the numbered words you wrote on page 74 to complete the passage.

The hippo is also known as the "river" _____.
                                                    1

A hippo's body is barrel shaped and _____ .
                                                 2

Hippos have _____ bellies, large heads, and
                        3

_____ legs. They live in _____,
         4   5

_____, and swamps.
         6

The hippo is a relative of camels, pigs, and _____.
                                                          7

Most of a hippo's day is spent laying _____ in the
                                                   8

_____. Sometimes, hundreds of hippos share a
         9

territory of water during the day. Hippos play, socialize, and

_____ in the water.
         10

A few hours after sunset, hippos leave the water to graze

on _____ by the light of the _____. So
        11   12

many hippos use the same path out of the water at dusk that it

becomes _____. It can be worn six-feet (1.5 m)
                  13

deep. _____ animals also use these paths to get to
              14

the water.

Answer Key

Page 3
Person: friend, Megan, pilot, parent;
Place: Indian Ocean, Neptune,
playground, South America; Thing:
cucumber, computer, refrigerator, shell;
Idea: love, imagination, happiness,
peace

Page 4
Common Nouns: doctor, liberty,
teammate, woman, artist, judge,
independence, river; Proper Nouns:
Kara, Ms. Prasad, Carlos Perez, Dr.
Dolby, Florida, France, Pacific Ocean,
Grand Canyon

Page 5
1. coaches; 2. sheep; 3. roofs;
4. mice; 5. donkeys; 6. shelves;
7. classes; 8. berries

Page 6
1. flock; 2. class; 3. committee;
4. fleet; 5. litter; 6. orchestra;
7. team; 8. crowd

Page 7
1. frogs'; 2. Marisa's; 3. boys';
4. neighbors'

Page 8
(First paragraph) Common nouns:
Cheetahs, speeds, miles (kilometers),
hour, cheetah, member, family,
Cheetahs; Proper nouns: Africa, Middle
East, India, Africa
(Second paragraph) Cheetahs' (second
sentence)
(Third paragraph) Plural nouns:
Cheetahs, antelopes, hares, cheetahs,
zebras, wildebeests, cheetahs;
Collective nouns: group, herd, prey,
prey

Page 9
1. I; 2. we, we; 3. I, him, me; 4. It;
5. They, we, it, them

Page 10
1. mine; 2. Her, his; 3. his; 4. their; 5. Its

Page 11
1. I, her; 2. you, our; 3. He, their;
4. They, her; 5. She, mine; 6. We, our;
7. he, mine; 8. He, my; 9. She, hers;
10. His, ours

Page 12
1. play; 2. counts; 3. hides; 4. crouches;
5. crawls; 6. jumps; 7. giggles; 8. climbs

Page 13
1. is; 2. are; 3. is; 4. are; 5. are; 6. is;
7. are; 8. are

Page 14
1. remain; 2. become; 3. appears;
4. seems; 5. feels; 6. smell; 7. looks;
8. become

Page 15
1. would → make; 2. are → making;
3. should → eat; 4. might → buy;
5. can → chop

Page 16
1. had learned; 2. are practicing; 3. will
be held; 4. is driving; 5. was packed;
6. am competing; 7. should win;
8. could win

Page 17
1. floats, PR; 2. watched, PA; 3. dance,
PR; 4. sharpens, PR; 5. bandaged, PA;
6. tumble, PR; 7. flicked, PA;
8. designed, PA

Page 18
1. wrote; 2. taught; 3. drew; 4. found;
5. spoke; 6. felt; 7. held; 8. bent; 9.
heard; 10. caught; 11. threw; 12. went

Page 19
1. did; 2. ran; 3. took; 4. went; 5. slept;
6. began; 7. wore; 8. flew

Page 20
1. take, I will take piano lessons.;

Answer Key

2. comes, Ivan will come to my house on Saturdays.; 3. are, You will be the line leader today.

Page 21

1. signed, past; 2. will golf, future; 3. snaps, present; 4. climbs, present; 5. will set, future; 6. rocked, past

Page 22

1. N; 2. V; 3. V; 4. N; 5. V; 6. N; 7. N; 8. V

Page 23

1. large, wrapped → package; 2. Many, tiny → ants, fallen → tree; 3. Some, bothersome → mosquitoes, screen → door; 4. both, dirty → socks, two, muddy → shoes; 5. One, spotted → dalmatian, noisy, red, fire → engine; 6. sharp → scissors, thick, brown → paper; 7. two, tart → lemons; 8. large, red → apple

Page 24

Answers will vary.

Page 25

the, an, a, a, The, the, The, The, A, the, a

Page 26

1. older, oldest; 2. softer, softest; 3. louder, loudest; 4. shorter, shortest; 5. smaller, smallest

Page 27

1. more popular; 2. most valuable; 3. more elevated; 4. most enormous; 5. most impressed

Page 28

1. Chocolate → ice cream, popular → dessert; 2. large, yellow, school → bus, excited → children; 3. white → rabbit, front → yard; 4. delicious → lasagna, ill → neighbor; 5. art → fair, amazing → drawings; 6. funny → movie, four, young → children; 7. fancy, red → shoes,

black, white → ribbons; 8. rusty, old → truck, heavy → rain; 9. lovely, white → house, long, bumpy → road; 10. large → raindrops, old, metal → roof

Page 29

1. adjective; 2. verb; 3. noun; 4. verb; 5. adjective; 6. noun; 7. verb; 8. noun

Page 30

1. quickly → closed; 2. frequently → plays; 3. quietly → worked; 4. slowly → jogged; 5. thoroughly → mixed; 6. carefully → unwrap ; 7. safely → arrived; 8. Bashfully → smiled

Page 31

1. early → had arrived; 2. very → excited; 3. often → stopped; 4. backward → walked; 5. Now → was packed; 6. tonight → will arrive; 7. tomorrow → will sleep; 8. later → will unpack

Page 32

1. later; 2. more gracefully; 3. highest; 4. more brilliantly; 5. louder

Page 33

1. well; 2. surely; 3. real; 4. good; 5. badly; 6. bad; 7. really; 8. sure

Page 34

1. everywhere → were scattered; 2. extremely → long; 3. here → place; 4. carefully, accurately → complete; 5. beautifully; 6. faster; 7. politely; 8. loudest

Page 35

1. of; 2. beside; 3. under; 4. in; 5. from; 6. in; 7. with; 8. in

Page 36

1. to school; 2. in the tree; 3. above the fence; 4. from our neighborhood; 5. under the porch, behind our house; 6. for the event; 7. to his mom; 8. in the trunk

Answer Key

Page 37

of the night sky, through the sky, in the dark, on the ground, in the air, with her wings, in the bottom, of her wing, around herself, into her own mouth, at any time, until better times come along, near a cave entrance, to the same cave

Page 38

Answers will vary, but may include:
1. Ava slept on the plane, but she did not sleep on the train.; 2. The pencil is old, but the eraser is new.; 3. Aidan plays basketball, and Taylor plays tennis.; 4. The pillow is soft, but the blanket is scratchy.; 5. Amira finished her math, but she did not finish her reading.

Page 39

1. ADJ; 2. CONJ; 3. V; 4. V;
5. PREP; 6. ADJ; 7. V; 8. PRO

Page 40

1. (4, 2, 3, 5, 1) The big dog barked loudly.; 2. (2, 3, 5, 4, 1) A very happy woman smiled.; 3. (2, 5, 3, 1, 4) The huge airplane landed cautiously.;
4. (5, 2, 1, 4, 3) An orange ball bounced high.; 5. (5, 2, 4, 3, 1) The large orchestra played beautifully.

Page 41

1. S; 2. S; 3. S; 4. F; 5. S; 6. S; 7. F; 8. F

Page 42

1. bridge; 2. shoelace; 3. cousin;
4. Diamonds; 5. dad; 6. list; 7. sink;
8. Marcus

Page 43

1. We; 2. He or She; 3. They; 4. they;
5. She

Page 44

1. scrunched; 2. bounced;
3. rustled; 4. will be; 5. paddled;
6. has written; 7. splattered; 8. ate

Page 45

1. Yellowstone is; 2. park has; 3. bears, bison can be found; 4. Thousands come; 5. family camped; 6. We enjoyed; 7. brother saw; 8. We will visit

Page 46

1. That puppy by the bench (circle puppy); 2. One canoe near the dock (circle canoe); 3. This parrot with the green head (circle parrot); 4. The brown mare (circle mare); 5. Several slimy earthworms (circle earthworms); 6. The open garbage can (circle can); 7. Frogs (circle Frogs); 8. Our crackling campfire (circle campfire)

Page 47

1. may stain Heather's shoes (circle may stain); 2. hoot softly for a meal (circle hoot); 3. guard the goals (circle guard); 4. fills the bird feeder every week (circle fills); 5. will gather all of the nuts from that tree (circle will gather); 6. quickly subtracts a page of math problems (circle subtracts); 7. carefully sews the button on his jacket (circle sews); 8. will attend the ceremony next Tuesday (circle will attend)

Page 48

1. Dustin's noisy movie distracted Krystal from her work.; 2. The box of tissues was emptied quickly.;
3. The old, rusty swing continues to be the children's favorite.; 4. Tyler loaded the back of the truck with plants.;
5. Some shiny marbles were scattered across the tile floor.; 6. Many important men signed the Declaration of Independence.; 7. Few tomato plants will survive the early morning frost.;
8. Three steep cliffs towered above the river.; 9. A remote-controlled car raced

Answer Key

along the sidewalk.; 10. The giant toad ate many insects.

Page 49
1. them; 2. us; 3. him; 4. it; 5. her; 6. it

Page 50
1. Daytona Beach, Fort Lauderdale, and Miami (circle and); 2. Tourists and residents (circle and); 3. Florida's population and industry (circle and); 4. Many farmers, miners, and fishermen (circle and); 5. Beaches, a warm climate, and mineral deposits (circle and); 6. Oranges, grapefruits, and tangerines (circle and); 7. Several famous theme parks and water parks (circle and); 8. The Atlantic Ocean and the Gulf of Mexico (circle and)

Page 51
1. walked and marched in the parade (circle and); 2. took hold of the rope and climbed it (circle and); 3. climbed the tree and jumped on the branches (circle and); 4. grabbed his backpack and ran for the door (circle and); 5. scurried and hid (circle and); 6. ran across the mat and flipped (circle and); 7. fell on the floor and rolled (circle and); 8. played games and sang songs (circle and)

Page 52
1. causes; 2. form; 3. strikes; 4. creates; 5. rejoice; 6. barks; 7. occur; 8. ruins

Page 53
1. wants; 2. jump; 3. wonder; 4. live; 5. knows; 6. uses; 7. write; 8. enjoy

Page 54
1. munches; 2. flies; 3. fixes; 4. lays; 5. hurries; 6. buzzes; 7. teaches; 8. plays

Page 55
1. sit; 2. slide; 3. are; 4. were; 5. fly; 6. live; 7. are; 8. enjoy

Page 56
1. interesting → book; 2. wonderful → aromas; 3. muddy → tractor; 4. tired → children; 5. empty → trailer; 6. squishy → dough; 7. sleepy → Ana; 8. fun → class

Page 57
1. I'll; 2. he's; 3. they're; 4. they've; 5. you'll; 6. she's; 7. I'd; 8. they'd

Page 58
1. I am; 2. You are; 3. They are; 4. You had; 5. I have; 6. she is

Page 59
1. ever; 2. anywhere; 3. anyone; 4. ever; 5. anything; 6. was; 7. anyone; 8. any

Page 60
1. IN (?); 2. IM (.); 3. D (.); 4. E (!); 5. IN (?)

Page 61
1. One, Albert Einstein; 2. Einstein, Ulm, Germany; 3. In, Einstein, University of Zurich; 4. He, Prague; 5. Albert Einstein, England, United States; 6. In, Einstein, American; 7. He, Princeton, New Jersey; 8. Albert Einstein, *Ideas*, *Opinions*

Page 62
1. The, Lewis, Clark, Expedition, United States; 2. The, Pacific Ocean; 3. In, May, Camp Dubois; 4. An, Indian, Sacagawea, Lewis, Clark; 5. They, Missouri River, Rocky Mountains; 6. Next, Columbia River

Page 63
1. Mr. Benjamin Franklin; 2. Mexican-American; 3. European; 4. Dr. John Kaplan; 5. Italian; 6. Mrs. Tanaka; 7. English; 8. Captain Sam Chadwick

Answer Key

Page 64

1. Aunt Jackie; 2. John F. Kennedy, U.S.; 3. Saturday, Dad, I, Yosemite National Park; 4. My, C. S. Lewis

Page 65

1. Nina, Ian, Kori, and I rode the bus.; 2. Her pen pal lives in Olympia, Washington.; 3. Our yogurt choices are cherry, strawberry, peach, or banana.; 4. Kim washed her face, brushed her teeth, and combed her hair.; 5. Mark was born in Halifax, Nova Scotia.; 6. Carrots, lettuce, spinach, and cucumbers are in the salad.

Page 66

1. Alaska became a state on January 3, 1959.; 2. On May 26, 2010, I went on a trip to Peru.; 3. The band is performing on Friday, June 2.; 4. My grandparents were married on June 26, 1971.; 5. Trisha was born on Sunday, January 6, 2002.; 6. Lee started kindergarten on Tuesday, August 27.; 7. Bailey will graduate on June 10, 2020, with an English degree.; 8. The program will be on Thursday, February 15.

Page 67

1. The huge, green house on Grant Lane is vacant.; 2. Jeremy and Jay are talented, experienced, professional skaters.; 3. Mom cooked a delicious, nutritious dinner.; 4. Finishing this project will be a long, complicated process.; 5. The shipmates watched the dull, gloomy sky.; 6. The creative, energetic, young drummer was the crowd favorite.; 7. The high, fluffy, white clouds filled the clear, blue, summer sky.; 8. After our long, exciting vacation, we returned to our peaceful, quiet neighborhood

Page 68

1. "Summertime" is a chapter in the book, A Year with Me.; 2. I want to read "No Bikes Allowed" in today's newspaper.; 3. The headline on this page says "Meteor Shower Tonight.";4. Irene played "Marching Along" on her flute.; 5. Zeb's favorite song is "High Hopes.";6. I love the poem "When Stars Come Out."

Page 69

1. "Please wait for me," Nicholas said.; 2. Josh said, "I think you should enter the contest."; 3. Liza asked, "What is your phone number?"; 4. Dad said, "Travis is at the recreation center today."; 5. "When will the parade begin?" asked the excited children.; 6. The toddler said, "Please read me a story."; 7. "May I speak with Mrs. Jung?" the caller asked.; 8. The salesperson explained, "This will just take a minute."

Page 70

1. There, week; 2. buy, new; 3. weigh, they're; 4. right, eight; 5. one, two, hours

Page 71

1. its; 2. through; 3. whole; 4. Its; 5. sent; 6. threw; 7. cent; 8. It's; 9. scent; 10. hole

Pages 72–75

Answers will vary.